POLITICS versus THE PEOPLE

Also by Derrick Arnott:

Social Domestic and Pleasure: Volume I
Spiderwize 2011. ISBN 978-1908026224

Accidental Millionaire: Volume II
Spiderwize 2011. ISBN 978-1908026309

STUDENTS can obtain a FREE copy of the original manuscript for *Politics versus the People*. See Part Seven.

POLITICS

versus

THE

PEOPLE

Then, Now... & Next?

Derrick Arnott

DB

DIADEM BOOKS

Politics versus The People: Then, Now…& Next?

Published by Diadem Books

For information, please contact:

Diadem Books
16 Lethen View
Tullibody
Alloa
FK10 2GE UK

www.diadembooks.com

ISBN: 978-1-326-03636-2

TABLE OF CONTENTS

Recommended reading available from the Electoral Reform Society:

PR Myths
A penny for your vote
Deal or No Deal
Turn out or turn off
The great local vote scandal
The Lottery Election
Women in Westminster
The 2015 Election Report

These can be downloaded free from the Electoral Reform Society website.

INTRODUCTION

BY **READING THIS BOOKLET** you will, in about thirty minutes' time, begin to understand why almost everybody in Britain is disillusioned and dissatisfied with our politics and politicians. You will also be encouraged to find that our broken system *can* be fixed – and how, with your help, this can be achieved.

Part One briefly looks at the evolution of citizens' suffrage, from Magna Carta in 1215 to votes for women in 1928. This will give you some idea of the task which faces those who continue to campaign for democratic emancipation.

Part Two examines government today and questions why we tolerate a system in which dishonesty and incompetence thrive.

Part Three analyses the constitutional significance of the 2015 general election.

Part Four focuses on what needs to happen to bring

about reform.

Part Five expounds upon an idealistic but not entirely unrealistic scenario, in which those who would benefit from reform could work together to bring it about.

Part Six speculates on what it would be like to live in a democratically governed Britain.

Our corrupt and inadequate politicians are endured by a frustrated and impotent electorate. **Part Seven** offers *you* the opportunity to play a part in changing this.

The data and information used is broadly accurate on the date of publication and where necessary has been adapted and simplified to achieve the booklet's objective, which is to play its part in the campaign for honest, competent and democratic government.

To find out more, see recommended reading, or visit:
www.electoral-reform.org
or
 www.unlockdemocracy.org

One

THEN

PERHAPS THE EARLIEST example of the devolution of power was the Magna Carta in 1215 signed by King John, which gave the barons a say in government and ended the absolute power of the monarchy.

In 1432 during the reign of the infant King Henry VI (crowned at 9 months old) the vote was officially granted to men who owned property worth more than forty shillings. This amounted to about 2% of the population.

The subsequent three centuries saw parliament develop and become more influential in government but a growing frustration among the people led to demands for the franchise to be extended.

Resisted by the establishment who saw this and the emergence of women's campaign groups as a threat to its power, democratic progress was not achieved easily and in 1819 on the site of St Peters Square in Manchester, what became known as the Peterloo Massacre took place when the Yeomanry were deployed to break up a peaceful demonstration and sixteen demonstrators, including a woman and a child, were reported to have lost their lives.

Similar events were taking place in France where seventeen thousand were officially executed and many more died in prison before their revolution, started in 1789, culminated in the guillotining of Louis XVI and Marie Antoinette and the overthrow of the monarchy in favour of a republic.

This gives us some idea of the lengths the establishment will go to in order to resist democratic progress and keep their stranglehold on power.

No doubt influenced by events across the channel and the growing pressure for reform at home, Lord Grey, the British Prime Minister, introduced a series of measures designed to pacify the reformers, leading to what was hailed as the "Great Reform Act" in 1832. However, since this extended the franchise only to men who owned property worth more than £10 it was hardly a dramatic change in the status quo and still left 85% of the people disenfranchised.

The establishment's grip on power was barely affected by this step since each voter was required to stand on a platform and announce his choice of candidate for all to see – and if his landlord or employer did not approve of his choice he faced eviction or dismissal. We shall see later how this expedient is still employed today by those in power.

Sustained pressure by the reformers, notably a group called The Chartists, led to a further Reform Act in 1872 known as the Secret Ballot Act following which men were finally able to vote without fear or favour – but only the select few.

A few years later the pressure for further reform led to all men over 18 getting the vote and then, in 1918, women over thirty with property rights and finally to all women over 18. Again this was a lengthy and hard fought campaign costing the life of Emiline Pankhurst, a leading suffragette.

At that point electoral and democratic evolution ceased and political power is now in the hands of a single party which is elected by a minority of the people under an unfair voting system.

Let us now look at how this functions.

Two

NOW

***P**OWER CORRUPTS... and absolute power... corrupts absolutely.*
Lord Acton (1834 – 1902)

So what exactly is democracy?

There seems to be no definitive definition. All governments claim that the system under which they operate is democratic. But then they would, wouldn't they?

But no matter how much they (the political establishment) pretend and would have us believe that we are a democracy, the reality is that we actually have more in common with a dictatorship.

Surely democracy should mean that the majority of the people get the government they want. But this is not the case under our "winner takes all" system where a single political party is able to impose its ideology on the people – even the thirty million people who didn't vote for it. Isn't that what dictators do?

Her Majesty's so-called "Official Opposition Party" has little or no influence on decision making. Constitutionally it is powerless to stop the ruling party, with an overall majority of seats, **but not of votes**, doing whatever it wants to because, quite undemocratically, it is given exactly the **absolute power** which Lord Acton warned us about. Consequently the Conservative and Labour parties have become obsessed with single party rule and have convinced themselves and their supporters that this is the only way a country can be governed. This narrow perception suits them of course. But it results in divisive and confrontational governance. One party may come up with an idea which is of obvious benefit to the country, yet the other party will immediately denounce it and make it into a party political issue. What is put in place by one government may be dismantled by the next. This will always be the case while the political establishment is obsessed with either/or single party government by two uncompromising parties bitterly opposed to each other. Little wonder progress is such a ponderous process.

You couldn't possibly run a successful company when half of the board of directors and its shareholders are constantly at loggerheads with the other half. Yet we expect a nation to function in such circumstances.

Unlike those who manage successful commercial enterprises, directors on the board of Great Britain plc (the government), don't need experience and skills in their jobs. They are often given important positions for other reasons (see later). What they **do** need is party loyalty and a talent for deception, denial and evasion. In other words they need to be good politicians.

The manner in which important matters of government are debated and decided is nothing short of farcical. The chamber itself, which is capable of seating only about one third of the total members, is divided, like a gladiatorial arena, into two "ends" from which the opposing parties we have entrusted with the welfare of our nation, hurl abuse at each other like overgrown schoolchildren.

Rarely do many of them actually turn up for work – something which would get the rest of us the sack. Instead they will "pair off" to cancel out each other's vote. Many of those who *are* present are merely there to make up the numbers. Instead of listening to or taking part in the debate, they lounge around in the members' bar drinking (and smoking, which is prohibited in every other bar in the country). When they hear the division bell ring to signify the end of the debate, they go along to the division lobby where they are instructed by their party whips to vote for or against the motion on an issue about which they often haven't a clue.

Failure to toe the party line can have serious consequences for rebellious MPs with minds of their own. The party whips have the power to destroy the political careers of dissenters. Hence our politicians live in fear of saying something which may displease the party hierarchy. **Often this can be simply telling the truth!**

A nation's citizens are entitled to expect that the politicians running their country are of the highest calibre, but there is much evidence that the process used for selecting candidates precludes this. Party loyalty all too often takes precedence over competence and the selection process leaves much to be desired. Cronies of the Party leader, irrespective of ability, are often given "safe seats" thus guaranteeing them certainty of election. So too are candidates foisted on the Party by their donors in return for financial support – a particularly disturbing form of blackmail. Around 40% of new candidates have probably worked with or are known personally to the selectors. This "old boys" network applies equally to both parties.

This is why more and more career politicians have replaced those with the experience and skills essential to understand the real world and who can contribute competently to the welfare of the nation.

It is inevitable under this incestuous selection culture that many of our MPs are "not fit for purpose".

An example of this and of the irrelevant, even disingenuous existence of some government departments, is encapsulated in the following story.

Before publishing this second edition of *Politics versus the People* a print proof version of the original draft was sent for comment to The Ministry for Political and Constitutional Reform. They did not respond directly.

Why not?

Could it be that this particular government department is little more than a quango, designed by the establishment to deceive us into believing that it actually takes reform seriously?

There wasn't even a Minister in charge of this Ministry. Apparently it used to have one but he had been put in charge of another department set up to ensure that the employment of illegal immigrants was stamped out. He was then forced to resign when, unbelievably – or maybe not so – it was discovered that he himself employed an illegal immigrant!

Really bright, talented and open-minded individuals – the ones who should be running the country – prefer to think for themselves. For this reason many do not enter politics. If you do not identify entirely and wholeheartedly with the doctrines of one of the major parties then it is almost impossible to become an MP. Under the present system it is a closed shop. Other parties, despite considerable popular support, rarely get their candidates elected even if they are more worthy than those of their opponents. Instead we have many second rate, often disreputable, MPs chosen by their parties for the wrong reasons. Party puppets are preferred to people with minds of their own.

After New Labour was created and Socialism abandoned in order for the party to become more electable and after the Conservatives modified their right-wing dogma for the same reason, both parties moved to the centre of politics. The voices of those MPs within the Conservative Party who still believed in old fashioned British values and those within new Labour who still believed in old fashioned Socialism, were effectively gagged by their party hierarchies in an effort to appeal to a broad base of voters in the quest for absolute power. Individual principles were subdued for the sake of party "unity".

Why was it left to UKIP and not the Eurosceptics within the Tory Party to object to EU rule? Where were the anti-privatization voices within New Labour in the 1990's? All we heard then was the "party line". Power has indeed compromised the principles of many within our political establishment.

In reality there are fundamental divisions within both main parties but the cracks have been papered over for the sake of political expediency. This unsatisfactory 'one size fits all state of affairs' exists because single party rule is engrained in our political culture.

Surely in a democracy it is important that opinions on vital issues are expressed and not suppressed? Surely the people would prefer to hear the honest opinions of their MPs instead of being fed a well-rehearsed "party line". Would it not be better if the Conservatives and the Eurosceptics were two separate parties? Would it not be better if New Labour and the Socialists were two separate parties? Would our democracy not be a much healthier one if this were the case?

Hypocrisy is not confined to the two main parties. Again, in 2010, power was preferred to principles. This time by the Liberal Democrats who, having campaigned for many years for proportional representation, finally found themselves in a position to demand it as a condition of their coalition with the Conservatives. This golden opportunity was tamely surrendered in exchange for the deputy leadership and a few seats in the Cabinet.

The main parties would like to think that we voters should fit neatly into two political categories – **but we don't.** The people's choice is being frustrated by our electoral system and, as we shall see later, by an unfair party funding mechanism. Frustrated too are all those many millions of supporters of minor parties which, despite having national appeal and support, are denied seats in parliament.

Our electoral system is heavily stacked in favour of a two-party establishment.

With only two realistic and equally unattractive choices the excitement has disappeared from politics and millions of those who do vote, do so on a "lesser of two evils" basis. Many vote for one of the main parties because their parents voted for it or because there is no other viable option or in the naïve and vain belief that a change of party in power will deliver the promised land!

In around four hundred constituencies the result is already known before the election takes place. So if you live in a "foregone conclusion" constituency, what is the point of voting for any other party if you know its candidate has no chance of being elected? What, indeed, is the point of another party having a candidate there in the first place? So why bother on polling day going through all the rigmarole of pretending that a democratic process is taking place?

By far the biggest electoral bloc is the 40% or so of the electorate who do not bother to vote or who vote tactically. The percentage is much greater at Local Authority level.

- Many because they do not trust the main parties.

- Many because their vote is meaningless unless they live in one of the few marginal seats which are the only ones that matter.

- Many because they find the contest between similar and equally discredited parties boring.

- Many because there isn't yet a party with which they can identify.

- Many because they are dismayed with the quality of candidates on offer.

- Many because they refuse to vote for their preferred party's candidate after he or she has been found acting dishonestly.

Members of parliament are allowed to remain in their jobs on full pay and pension rights when they have been found to be dishonest.

- When they fiddle expenses.

- When they accept bribes.

- When they and their parties are influenced (some would say bribed) by favour seeking lobbyists for personal or party advantage.

- When they use their important positions to cover up their unlawful sexual activities with young children.

- When they are convicted of criminal offences

Little wonder we distrust political parties who, by failing to expel the rascals, condone such behaviour.

How can government expect the people to behave honestly when they themselves set such an appalling example?

There are of course some honest hard working politicians. But, to quote Henry Kissinger:

"90% of politicians get the other 10% a bad name."

Honest, impartial and ethical government, given the fragility of human nature, is not possible when political parties can achieve absolute power against the wishes of most people and are funded by external interests who will expect something in return.

He who pays the piper calls the tune!

These outside interests include the EU which has devised a back door mechanism by which they are able to fund the main parties (but not minor parties) to the tune of millions of pounds. In 2013 the EU funded three political organizations – the Tory AECR (£1.4 million), the Lib Dem ALDE (£2.23 million) and Labour's European Socialists (£4.99 million).

How is it possible to have a fair and impartial

debate on EU membership – and a meaningful referendum – when the establishment is being paid to make sure we don't have one?

Should anyone be surprised that people have little respect for politicians, have disengaged from politics and that over a period of fifty years turnouts at general elections slumped from 83.6% to 59.4%? They did however increase in 2015, probably due to a combination of the popularity of emerging alternative parties, tactical voting and vote rigging (see later).

Only three other world democracies have lower turnouts.

Those with the highest turnouts (over 90%) do not operate the same electoral system as ours. In fact only a handful of them do. This should say something to us.

As long as our political parties have an opportunity to cling on to power under an outdated electoral system, the people cannot be expected to find the government of Britain acceptable. Yet our political establishment stubbornly defends this unfair system because it fears that a fairer system may be a threat to its power – just as the establishment has done for thousands of years. Why should either party want to change a system, even if it is unfair, which has enabled them to take turns in government – six times each since 1924? How can a nation have a long-term development strategy in such circumstances?

How can you expect to have a happy family when every five years mam and dad take turns at having custody of the children?

Political government has been likened to a dysfunctional family. To make the kids love them (vote for them) each parent (each Party) will promise them more pocket money (higher incomes and benefits) and more toys (material possessions). To buy these the parent (the government) borrows money from a loan shark (the International Monetary Fund).

Included in everyone's tax payments is £2,000 every year in order to pay the government's £43 billion annual interest on the money borrowed.

Even the two main parties who benefit from the electoral system which bestows upon them absolute power of government, occasionally find it difficult to justify and from time to time will offer us some token gestures – as Lord Derby did a hundred years ago.

...like a referendum, not on proportional representation, but on a watered down AV version which few of us could be bothered to understand and even fewer of us saw as a solution.

...and like Labour's vote-catching promise in its 1997 election manifesto which it obviously had no intention of keeping. *"An independent Commission on voting will... recommend a proportional alternative to the first past the post system."*

...and like the Conservatives' intention to change constituency imbalances – not because they are unfair but because it will benefit their party at the polls.

Surely these weren't Lord Derby style attempts to placate those who were urging reform - were they? Of course they were.

Three

2015

REALISING that falling turnouts were a threat to its credibility, certain desperate steps were taken by the establishment prior to the 2015 general election starting with the Fixed Term Parliament Act.

Large amounts of taxpayers' money were then spent trying to persuade people to vote.

Arrogantly assuming that the problem was simply voter apathy and not its own failings, the establishment introduced voter registration days which were largely ignored. It either failed to realize or, more likely, chose not to realize that it and not the electorate was the problem

In another desperate attempt to "reinvigorate our democracy", on demand postal voting was introduced. This ill-conceived idea was labelled by a top judge as "being open to fraud on an industrial scale" and sure enough vote rigging was rampant in some vulnerable marginal constituencies.

Prior to the election all the pundits were convinced that we would have a hung parliament and maybe a constitutional crisis, the cause of which could be laid squarely at the door of an unsuitable and obsolescent voting system.

Calls for electoral reform gathered momentum.

Alas, the hopes of the reformists were dashed when a Conservative government was returned to office with an overall majority. Democratic evolution was the loser in this election.

There is, of course, nothing new in this, since for centuries people who didn't vote for the winning Party have, in effect, been denied a say in the affairs of their country.

The difference however in this election was the support demonstrated for the alternative parties UKIP, the SNP and the Greens.

The table below shows just how irrational and

undemocratic our voting system is.

UKIP......3,881,121 votes (12.6%)......1 seat (0.154% of the total)
SNP........1,454,436 votes (4.7%)......56 seats (8.6% of the total)
Green......1,157,613 votes (3.8%) ....1 seat (0.154% of the total)

So SNP, with more than 3.5 million fewer votes than UKIP and Green, end up with 54 more seats. Yet we are told that we live in a democracy!

The SNP factor was potentially a time bomb since they could quite easily have found themselves holding the balance of power (possibly with Labour) thus creating a situation which enabled an exclusively regional party, whose desire was to break up the UK, dictating policy affecting the 39,641,723 (96.46%) people who didn't vote for it.

If this alarming prospect could have become reality in 2015 what's to stop it happening in future elections? The emphatic – and only – answer to this question is **proportional voting.** Had this been in place in 2015 the SNP would still have won 30 seats in parliament but not enough to allow them to wield such dangerous power because other emerging parties would have won 168 seats too, resulting in a fair, balanced and much more democratic British government.

In contrast the Conservatives with 11,300,303 votes (37% of the vote but only 27.5% of the electorate) won 330 (50.77%) of the seats and Labour with 9,344,328 votes (30%) won 232 (35.69%) of the seats.

So, it took nearly 4 million votes to elect one single UKIP MP, well over 1 million votes to elect a Green MP, but only 34,243 votes to elect a Conservative MP and only 25,972 votes to elect a SNP MP.

Even based on these figures it is abundantly clear that our voting system is a shambles but the actual situation is even worse since it is likely that UKIP and particularly the Greens would have received many more votes if their candidates stood any chance of winning. The figures are also distorted because of two other factors inherent in the present system –tactical voting (estimated at 9%) and postal vote rigging.

Based on the statistics above, here is what a proportional government would have looked like in seat numbers:

Conservative...	...	...	242
Labour	...	...	208
UKIP	...	...	80
Lib Dem ...	...	...	47
SNP	...	...	30
Green	...	...	28
Others	...	...	13

It should be borne in mind however that with an opportunity to match their votes more closely with a party of their choice, many more people would turn out to vote and many traditional voters would surely defect from the main parties if alternative parties were more likely to win seats in parliament. A true proportional government is likely therefore to be quite different to the above, particularly if new parties are formed (see Part Six).

The result of this election was not all bad news for the reformists. In an unprecedented move by UKIP, the SNP, the Greens, Lib Dems and Plaid Cwymru, these parties put their differences aside and joined forces to protest against the inequity of our electoral system. Could this be the first sign that those who are thus unfairly discriminated against (and this includes most of the electorate) may be prepared to unite in a common cause and fight together for the sake of democracy?

The picture below shows the leaders of these parties with Katie Ghose, Chief Executive of the Electoral Reform Society and other reformists delivering a 500,000 signature petition at 10 Downing Street.

Four

NEXT

POLITICAL BRITAIN is not enjoying the best of health. It is suffering from a particularly nasty virus – a first past the post (FPTP) electoral system.

FPTP serves only one purpose, which is to keep the two main parties in power. It must be scrapped and replaced by proportional voting, under which the anomalies and inequity of FPTP are eliminated and **political parties are allocated seats in parliament in proportion to the number of votes they actually receive at the polls.**

Calls for a reform of our electoral system have so far been subjugated by the political establishment helped by a passive and brainwashed public. The two main parties want to keep it that way, although there are a number of their MPs who have openly declared and demonstrated their support for reform. Their parties so far have raised no objection to their harmless posturing but bearing in mind that they have sworn allegiance to parties who are opposed to reform, it remains to be seen how serious and principled these individuals are, should their pro-reform vote ever be needed in parliament. Would they defy their party whips? Would they be prepared to jeopardize their chances of candidate selection or promotion? Or would their principles be abandoned for the sake of party loyalty?

If a campaign for electoral reform is to succeed, the support of existing MPs would of course be important. Whether this could be relied on is another matter. Equally, if not more important, would be to harness the energies of those candidates who have tried and failed to win seats.

Important too, indeed essential, is the need to get the message across to a largely disinterested public who for generations have been used to the country's traditional voting methods. To do this the pro-reform arguments must be presented in a decisive, persuasive and concise manner – and certainly in a more forceful and dramatic way than hitherto.

The two fairest alternative electoral systems are thought to be STV (the Single Transferrable Vote) and

PR (Proportional Representation).

Under STV two or more constituencies would be amalgamated into one multi-seat electoral district. Candidates would be elected by voters marking on their ballot papers a number 1 against their first choice candidate, number 2 against their second choice and so on. There are a number of fairly complicated formulae for allocating the votes and counting them is a lengthy process. The author for example, in his bid to be elected to the Council of the Electoral Reform Society, was eliminated at stage 13 of the 20 counts. One can only imagine what a protracted affair a post-general election count would be.

One argument for STV is that it would retain a local link between voters and MPs. However, to eliminate the flaws in single seat constituency voting, the districts would need to be quite large, involving perhaps dozens of the old constituencies, which tends to diminish this pro-STV argument. Small districts favour the main parties and may still provide them with safe seats into which they could "parachute" their preferred candidates.

PR is more straightforward. People would simply cast

their votes for the party of their choice and, for the purpose of electing a National Assembly, the votes would be counted nationally. Non-establishment parties would then stand a much better chance of their candidates being elected. Unless, under STV, the districts were very large, PR would seem to produce a more exploitation proof model of democratic government. It also has the huge advantage of being easier for the reformers to "sell" to a largely disinterested and sceptical public, most of whom already know what PR is. With STV much of the reformers' energies would be consumed by explaining how it works.

The personal contact between voters and MPs can be retained, indeed improved, by devolution to the regions.

An argument used against proportional voting is that it may give "unacceptable" parties a say in government. Unacceptable to whom? Certainly not the supporters of such parties. Those who would use this argument are, in effect, saying that their own views are okay to be represented but not those of a section of their fellow citizens. Do these bigots want democracy or do they want semi-democracy? If you truly believe in democracy you must accept it for what it is. If you want it on your terms then it's not democracy.

Both STV and PR have merit. The important thing is that the main obstacle to democratic government – individual single seat constituencies – is removed, and both systems, to a lesser or greater extent, aim to do this.

There are countless reasons why FPTP must be confined to history.

Why does the appointment of our government have to be an "either/or" choice? Why should popular minor parties (and therefore their supporters) be excluded from having their say in government?

It is unacceptable that we must be ruled by a single political party which around four out of five of us don't want and don't vote for.

It is absurd that a party with fewer votes than its opponent can actually win an election.

It is crazy that a constituency with an electorate of 21,837 elects one MP and another with an electorate of 110,924 can only elect one MP too.

It is nonsense that one party needs nearly 4 million votes to give them an MP and another just a few thousand.

It is wrong that unscrupulous people can abuse the system by vote rigging.

It is sad that people have to vote tactically because the party of their choice has no chance of success.

It is scandalous that voting is pointless for around 22 million people who live in "safe seats" where the result is known before the election.

It is even more scandalous that many of these seats are "contested" not by worthy candidates, but are bestowed on puppets "recommended" by donors to party funds or by cronies of party leaders.

These are but a few of many examples of our crazy electoral system. In fact it is hard to find anything about FPTP which is fair, sensible and logical. The situation at local government level is in even more urgent need of reform.

In the name of democratic evolution we must aim to achieve a system of government which is not dominated by two parties.

The people must be given a meaningful choice.

In the age of parties before people and with the political establishment firmly entrenched and determined to keep it that way it is hard to see them introducing a fairer system which jeopardizes their stranglehold on power. They pay lip service to reform but in reality will resist it to the death.

There are a number of myths perpetrated by the establishment parties, designed to dissuade us from adopting PR. These are examined – and exploded – in the excellent publication *PR Myths* available from The Electoral Reform Society.

An objection put forward by the establishment desperate to keep FPTP, is that the people will not have access to their local MP. But since only a minority of the electorate are likely to have voted for him or her, the rest of them may not feel comfortable seeking help or advice from someone to whom they are politically opposed and may be therefore disinclined to do so – if indeed they are lucky enough to have an MP who actually spends time in the constituency. There is no obligation on MPs to do so.

Under a regional proportional system there would usually be an MP of the party of your choice available locally and almost certainly a Regional Assembly member.

If they were really honest, the main, if not the only, objection by the establishment parties to PR is that it would threaten their power. They will never admit this of course. Instead they would have us believe the myths, one of which is that it would lead to weak government. How dare they claim that truly democratic government will be weak when in reality the very opposite is true.

The only things which *would* be weaker under PR are the absolute power bestowed upon a single party and the power of the party whips who force MPs to always toe the party line, even against their better judgment or their consciences. This 19th Century practice which threatened the homes and jobs of people who did not vote as required by their landlords or employers, has no place in a democratic 21st Century parliament.

- Both parties, fearing bad press, toady to the media. Is this strong government?

- Both parties are afraid of standing up to the unelected bureaucrats of Brussels. Is this strong government?

- Both parties are in the pockets of their benefactors – donors to party funds. Is this strong government?

- Both parties introduce "stealth taxes" (with all the associated bureaucratic costs) because they are scared of what their opponents would say if they did it in a more straightforward way. Is this strong government?

- Both parties are paranoid about making decisions affecting marginal constituencies. Is this strong government?

The main energies of our MPs are focused on protecting their majorities so decisions are influenced not objectively but by how many votes the decisions may gain or lose and on local issues they depend on which constituency is involved. People who live in marginal constituencies are much more likely to get their own way than those in "safe" ones.

Strong government means making decisions for the long-term benefit of the country, not for short-term political advantage. These decisions may not be universally popular and may mean that a few votes are lost in a few marginal seats. Under FPTP this is often enough to make the difference between success and failure at a general election. Consequently some important or controversial issues are simply ignored.

The national debt is a graphic example of weak governance.

We simply cannot continue indefinitely to live beyond our means. Inevitably there must be a day of reckoning. This is the legacy which successive governments have been content to leave to future generations whose future prosperity is being sacrificed on the altar of political power. This will always be the case when the prize of absolute power is achievable in a two-horse race between two parties who, at election time, are prepared to plunge the nation further into debt by bribing the electorate with promises we cannot afford.

The party with the biggest election budget is more likely to win. Pre-election time is an opportunity for selfish party donors to screw more concessions out of the parties for their own benefit and to the detriment of the people.

Thus the elected party begins its term of office with one hand tied behind its back. It must find the money to fund its promises to the electorate – and it has made this difficult to do because of its promises to the donors who helped it to win.

To win votes a party must promise to give more than its opponent. Once elected as a result of these irresponsible and unrealistic promises, the party must either renege on them or borrow more. This means more debt for future generations. Does the party care about this? No. It has achieved its priority which is to win the election at all costs. Such is the danger of single party rule.

If the state promises too much it creates unrealistic

expectations. It creates a dependency among its citizens. To avoid an inevitable economic catastrophe it is vital that a future government must reverse this pattern of expectation and dependency and encourage individuals to earn the benefits of prosperity instead of relying on the state. Unless something is done, expect a reaction from taxpayers as fewer of them are expected to support an increasing number of dependents.

Which of today's parties is willing to shoot itself in the foot by seriously addressing such important issues? This is why the concept of single party rule must be abandoned and replaced by a more responsible form of government.

The discontent of the people and the pressure for change from bodies like the Electoral Reform Society is condescendingly listened to but it is ineffective in the face of the might of the main parties. Maybe those millions of people who boycott the polling booths are doing democracy a favour. Perhaps if turnouts fell below 50% some half-hearted changes may be made – but don't hold your breath.

Maybe the best hope for immediate change is another

"hung" parliament in which the party or parties holding the balance of power agree to a coalition but only on condition that a fairer electoral system is introduced, which is what the Lib Dems should have done in 2010.

There is another possibility.

The Electoral Reform Society, whose preferred voting system is the single transferrable vote (STV), has been striving to achieve reform for more than a century – **but we still have FPTP.** The Society's brief is limited to campaigning and lobbying for reform, not for direct action. Perhaps it is time for a more radical approach to the problem.

Repairs to our broken electoral system can only be achieved with the approval of parliament. This is not going to happen whilst it is dominated by two political parties who are anti-reform. No amount of campaigning is likely to change this. Only when their power is under threat will these parties take action.

Nobody has taken the issue forcefully into the political arena. Nobody has seriously given the people the chance to clean up politics, despite the rhetoric.

Perhaps the time is right for a new movement or party to enter the political arena to promote political reform. It would not need a lengthy manifesto containing unachievable promises that cannot realistically be kept. It would simply need to emphasize the inadequacies of the present system and the advantages of government after PR. These would include coming to terms with the fact that the one-party dictatorial style of government which enables it to impose its dogma on the people without a democratic mandate, would have to be abandoned in favour of a more mature and honest approach to party politics.

Should the reform movement gain momentum and become a threat to the political establishment, the reformers will need to have plenty of resolve to survive the 21st Century equivalent of the Peterloo Massacre!

Five

2020

IN PART THREE we described the unique spectacle of five political parties, who only a few days earlier had been locked in battle against each other, joining forces to protest against the common enemy – FPTP.

We now relate a fanciful version of what happened next. Call it wishful thinking if you like.

Although we were spared a constitutional nightmare on this occasion, 2015 had exposed dangerous flaws in our electoral system. This attracted much speculation and comment in the media and raised awareness among the people.

To take advantage of this awareness and signs that there may be an appetite for change among the electorate, let us suppose that a politically neutral, single issue party has been formed to contest the 2020 general election. Its manifesto is simple – to scrap FPTP and individual constituencies and to introduce proportional voting.

The party activists sought the backing of the various groups and individuals, including those within the main parties, who advocate and campaign for change. They then approached UKIP and the Green Party whose energies had been largely wasted in contesting 2015 which produced for them a mere two seats in parliament.

This is why these parties along with some Liberal Democrats, SNP and Plaid Cymru had joined the reformists in their protest at 10 Downing Street.

The new Reform Party suggests to these parties that their ideological aspirations should be postponed and instead of contesting the next election as opponents, which plays right into the hands of the establishment parties and the Conservative Party in particular, some form of alliance should be considered.

Talks between the parties took place and progressed

well since they recognized only too well that successful reform would enable them to have a greater say in future government.

An Alliance for reform was proposed to replace the Reform Party.

The Lib Dems who had long advocated reform, were invited to lend their support and so too were the anti-establishment SNP and Plaid Cymru.

The movement gained momentum and it became clear that the Alliance may enjoy some success at the polls.

Whilst Labour in the past had refused to countenance a change in the voting system there were signs that their attitude may be changing. There was a hint of this in the party's 2015 manifesto which included a promise of *"A people led Constitutional Convention to debate the future of UK governance"*.

After its disappointment at the polls in 2015, many in the Labour Party began to fear the prospect of many years in the wilderness of opposition. The likelihood of continued dominance by the SNP in Scotland and the probability of the Conservatives redrawing constituency boundaries in their favour did little to allay these fears, particularly after the election of a far left leader.

However it had not been lost on the Party that on a proportionate vote in 2015 they would have secured only 24 seats fewer than they did. Nor had it gone unnoticed that the Conservatives would have fared much worse with 89 fewer seats.

Like UKIP, the Lib Dems, the Greens, SNP and Plaid Cymru, what would they have to lose by throwing their weight behind a reform movement which was rapidly gaining popular support? Like these other parties Labour too may have something to gain from such an alliance and whilst it may not give them the possibility of overall control in the future, it may well result in this being denied to the Conservatives too.

Was the writing on the wall for the demise of single party rule? Was this an opportune time for the Labour Party to make history and support the campaign for reform?

Talks with the other alliance partners were initiated and a temporary agreement was reached that the 2020 election should be contested in cooperation with each other. A strategy was worked out and a tactical deployment of each party's resources and candidates was agreed, its objective being to oust the Conservatives and form a coalition until electoral reform was achieved, after which each party would be able to contest future elections with the advantage of proportional voting.

The polls suggested that the appetite for reform among voters was overwhelming. Finding themselves increasingly isolated, the Conservatives eventually capitulated.

Thus the Electoral Reform Act was introduced a couple of years into the 2020 parliament. It was an historic moment in British politics and a triumph for democracy.

Six

2040

NOW LET US TAKE A GLIMPSE of Britain twenty years after the reformers had succeeded in replacing first past the post with proportional voting.

Parliament is no longer based in Westminster and the building is now a museum and tourist attraction.

It has been dragged kicking and screaming into the 21st Century and a new state of the art purpose-built assembly has been constructed outside the capital which can actually accommodate *all* members. This was essential because they must now turn up and take part in debates before they are allowed to vote. They no longer have an excuse not to "turn up for work" because their constituency roles have now been devolved to Regional Assemblies.

The new National Assembly complex includes

accommodation, restaurants and other facilities for the use of members, their families and visitors. No more expensive flats in London and massive expenses claims. Being an MP is now a serious job without the glamour of previous eras.

Members are subjected to a strict code of conduct and ethics, any breach of which results in immediate loss of office and replacement by the next candidate on the list (see later). A lifetime ban on their participation in politics is also imposed.

If such a code had existed 30 years earlier there would have been a by-election every fortnight!

In order to ensure that central government does not become too remote from local issues there is a central government Minister for each region and representatives from Regional Assemblies are allocated debating time at the National Assembly and vice versa. Similarly, local authorities may send representatives, with voting rights, to Regional Assemblies. Certain times are also allocated for individual members of the public to raise questions.

Individual constituencies for the purpose of national

voting have been scrapped. The number of seats in the National Assembly will fluctuate according to population. One seat is allocated per 100,000 people on the electoral register, thus ensuring that the inconsistencies of the old constituency imbalances will not recur and that the size of the Assembly is appropriate to the workload.

Also under debate will be the suggestion that on certain issues, members' votes in the Assembly should be by secret ballot – decisions involving the deployment of our armed forces for example.

The whole ethos of government is changed. Democratising the voting system has enabled the voice of the people to play an important part in the process of government, which is no longer dominated by one or two parties. Other parties need to secure only a small percentage of the vote in order to win seats on the National and Regional Assemblies. No single party has been able to grab absolute control of government. After some failed early attempts at coalitions in order to power share, all parties have had to learn how to debate issues sensibly and to accept that a majority vote represents the wishes of the people and not the doctrine of one party.

Debate is not always confined to the elected national and regional members. Experts on particular issues and others with vested interests in the issues, are invited to openly address the assembly. No more furtive lobbying behind closed doors.

The demise of single party autocracy spelled the end of the "PM's cronies and cash for peerages" era. Meritocracy, not favours, favouritism and party loyalty is now the criteria for selecting members of the Second Chamber (previously the House of Lords).

Multi-Party government is gradually removing the obstacles which for many years delayed the reform of the House of Lords, which had become little more than a political battleground and a farcical "numbers game" with successive parties determined to ensure that their sympathisers outnumbered those of their political opponents so that their own legislation would be enacted without too much opposition, thus negating what surely should be the *raison d'etre* of a second chamber.

To make it a truly effective and credible part of governance the second chamber is being purged of its political dominance, since no single part is now able to bulldoze its own preferences into ermine gowns.

Because during the old single party rule era the House of Lords was the only constitutionally effective means of opposing unacceptable government legislation, albeit within limitations, calls for appointed Peers to be replaced by elected ones were sensibly resisted. Instead an independent selection model is being developed, the aim being to ensure that the second chamber has a majority of non-politically appointed or elected Peers and is made up of citizens who have proved themselves not as political allies, but as elder statesmen and women with no political allegiances to cloud their judgement.

Legislation can then be scrutinized objectively rather than politically.

Perhaps the most important change and the one welcomed most by the people was the quality and integrity of our politicians. Most are now individuals who are selected on merit rather than cronies being given safe seats on the whims of party leaders, or who are foisted on the Parties by those who bribe them with financial support.

Under the "List" system (see below) the selection of useless hangers on is a thing of the past since the suitability of a party's candidate nominations is carefully scrutinized by the voters, the media and opposing parties. The quality of the candidates on offer and not vague promises, is what the electorate will judge the party on.

As a result of this the profile of our MPs has changed. Political backgrounds are less important than hitherto. Candidates are generally individuals whose achievements in life, in public service, the professions and commerce look good on a party's list of candidates. Most have chosen to enter politics, not to espouse political dogma or for prestige, having already achieved this in their pre-political careers, but because they have a desire to offer the public the benefit of their wealth of experience and skills. They have brought a maturity to parliament with their willingness to work together for the benefit of people not party in a more practical and less ideological manner.

Much debate is taking place to find a suitable wording for a proposed British Constitution of the sort that exists in a republic. A 75% majority is required to approve decisions of such magnitude.

Party funding has been severely curtailed and regulated. After a party's first five years in existence, donations are limited to £1000 per annum and must come from individual and not corporate sources. Instead, each party is paid a sum of money for each vote it receives. This was considered a small price for the exchequer to pay in return for independent politics. In effect the traditional donors to party funds have been replaced by the people. The voters are now the pipers who call the tunes!

Before recommending the type of proportional electoral system to be adopted, the various models of the world's civilized nations had been studied and the one considered to be the fairest, the most likely to result in ethical politics and the most acceptable to the people and to the reformers whose campaigning had succeeded in bringing about change, was the PR List System, suitably modified for the UK.

All parties, prior to a general election, are required to submit for scrutiny a list of candidates in order of preference, with full details of their qualities, experience (not necessarily politically), personal circumstances, achievements, business interests and their misdeeds, including criminal convictions. They must provide, in effect, a CV for each candidate, setting out his or her suitability to represent the voters and to run a successful nation. Parties would identify in their lists those candidates who would be given special responsibility for individual regions or districts, thus retaining the local link between MP and voter.

The system works like this. If a party receives a percentage of the national vote (say 10%) to give it a similar percentage of the seats available (say fifty) then the first fifty candidates on its list would be elected.

This system is designed to ensure that only candidates with a degree of integrity and suitability acceptable to the electorate are included in the list. To do otherwise would be electoral suicide since it would attract unwelcome scrutiny and criticism by the media, the opposing parties and the voters.

How many of our current crop of MPs, we wonder, would the parties now dare to include in *their* lists?

As well as the curtailment of lobbying and bribes, the inclusion by some of the parties in their candidate lists, and therefore in government, of people with practical experience of business and commerce has resulted in naïve and gullible government departments no longer being "soft touches" when it comes to awarding government contracts and has led to much tighter controls in government spending and tougher negotiations on government contracts which are no longer awarded irresponsibly on political grounds by people with little or no business background or in return for "favours". Each tender is subjected to strict scrutiny by professionally experienced members. Before being awarded a contract a company is required to provide performance guarantees, both by its directors personally and by its parent company. In some cases bank guarantees are called for. Where it is thought prudent, a member of the government is placed on the board of directors in a watchdog capacity. Sometimes a share stake by the government is insisted upon.

These simple accountability measures ensure that companies and their directors are no longer tempted to use our money, hide behind their limited liability status, run away with impunity and then at a later date discretely reward personally the MPs who assisted them in ripping us off.

Some on the right of politics complained that this amounted to back door nationalization and those on the left thought that it did not go far enough. But these sensibly negotiated arrangements have created profitable partnerships and added to the prosperity of UK plc.

The people have benefited in many ways from multi party government. Crime is reduced and the nation's health is improved for example. With the big prize of single party autocracy gone, so has the fear of a backlash from big business and the media to the imposition of regulation upon them. Government can no longer be persuaded to turn a blind eye in exchange for promises of party funding and favours.

Prime time TV slots have been commandeered by government for public service announcements. These include exposing scams, showing CCTV footage of criminal activities, health warnings, lifestyle advice and much to the dismay of some TV channels, identifying spurious and inaccurate claims by advertisers. The food and drink industry has been forced to replace its unhealthy products with less harmful ones.

With the prize of absolute single party power depending on a few marginal constituencies, previous governments, fearful of the political consequences, were terrified of acknowledging past errors. This is no longer the case and in a move to improve multicultural harmony the multi-party British government offered an unreserved apology to the Muslim community for its ill-advised violation of Muslim lands, thus removing some tension within the community.

After some initial and inevitable teething problems and sabotage tactics by the old parties, the British government is now a role model to the world with its balance of national self interest and concern for others. Prudent management without political influence has produced budget surpluses which are used to provide better services for its citizens and aid for poorer countries. This is done out of earned wealth not false borrowed wealth.

We now have a government with a hard head but a

soft heart.

But most importantly, with the demise of career politicians and their replacement by competent candidates, selected for their ability to run a country and not their willingness to be political party puppets, the people's respect for politics is restored.

Let us at this point take a hypothetical view of the constitution of a future government.

As well as the old parties there is now a Tory breakaway Party led by the Eurosceptics and a separate Socialist Party.

With only 100,000 votes nationwide needed to elect a candidate, PR had paved the way for some minor parties to flourish and for new ones to emerge, but to discourage frivolous participation in elections certain safeguards are being considered. One is that a party will need to secure a minimum number or share of the votes in order to have its candidates elected.

One of the new entrants into the political arena, the WIGs (Women in Government), is perhaps destined to be the country's largest and most powerful political force. Could this be the final stage in the emancipation of women?

An opportunity has also been created for minority and even extremist groups to be recognized and represented.

True democracy is about, or should be about, voices being heard. Far better for extreme groups to have a democratic way to promote their aims instead of taking part in violent demonstrations or terrorism. As Voltaire the French Philosopher so rightly said:

"I may disagree strongly with what you say – but I will fight to the death for your right to say it."

How can anyone who believes in free speech and equal rights possibly disagree with that?

*　　*　　*

Is this fairyland?

Can it be achieved?

Many will have their doubts. But had the same

question been asked of the common man centuries ago, or of the pre-suffragette women in the 19th Century, or of the barons before Magna Carta, many would have had doubts too.

The establishment may have been able to procrastinate and postpone reform – but it has never been able to stop it. Future and more enlightened generations will make sure of that.

Seven

JOIN THE PARTY

DO YOU THINK that a single issue Reform/PR Party and/or an Alliance of pro-reform parties and organisations should contest the next general election?

Might you vote for it?

Might you join such a Party or Organisation?

Might you consider being a supporter, activist or candidate?

Might you be a suitable officer, candidate or even leader for the Party?

If your answer is YES to any of these questions or you think you could be involved in any other way, please simply email YES with your home COUNTY or REGION to prparty@gmx.co.uk and if there is sufficient interest you will be contacted and invited to an inaugural meeting prior to establishing the Party/Movement so that you can be involved in its foundation.

Please be patient. It may not be possible to respond to your email until the extent of the response has been assessed.

STUDENTS: email FREEMS to **prparty@gmx.co.uk** and we will reply attaching a free copy of the manuscript for this booklet.